THIS NOTEBOOK
— BELONGS TO —

100

questions to enhance your relationship with your kids.

By asking the right questions, we can start a great conversation about dreams, emotions, clever ideas or hidden problems.

After a few questions from this book, children will be drawn into play and their natural curiosity and creativity will be awakened! :)

This book can accompany you everywhere: at home, on a walk, in the car or on a trip.

It will be also a true time capsule after 10 or 20 years.

Get to know each other even better!

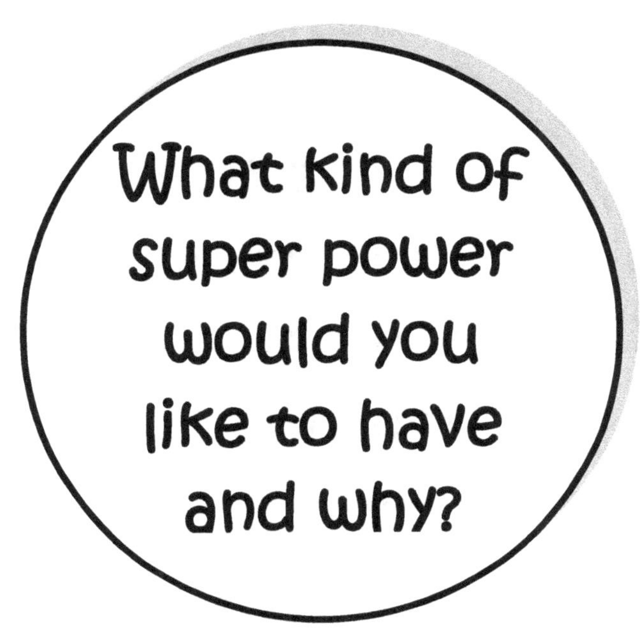

What kind of super power would you like to have and why?

What is the
coolest thing
you have
learned
recently?

If the internet,
TV and radio
were suddenly
turned off,
what would you
do?

What do you like to do best when you are with your best friend?

What kind of
wild animals
do you like?
Draw them on
the next page!

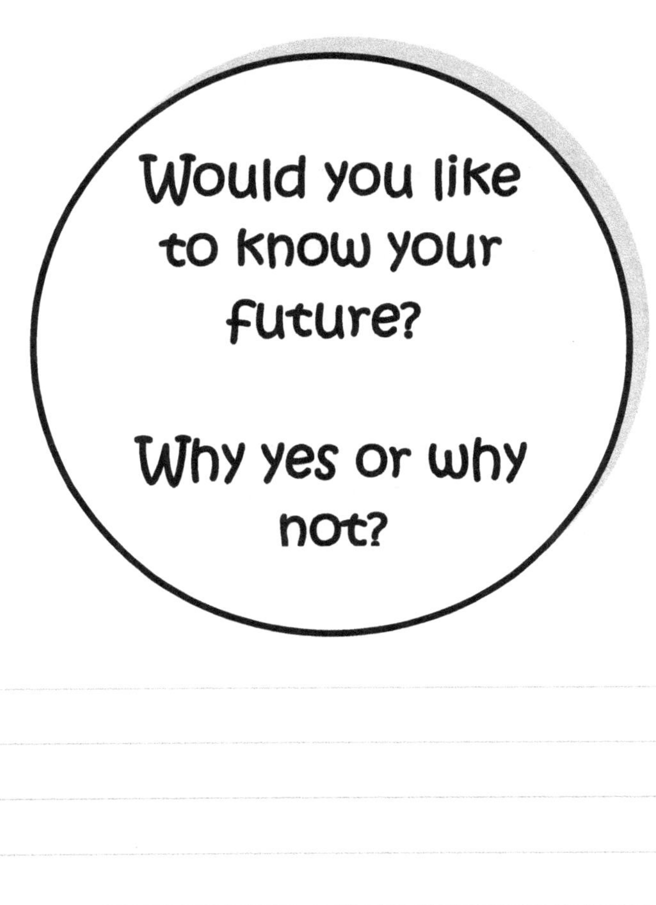

Would you like to know your future?

Why yes or why not?

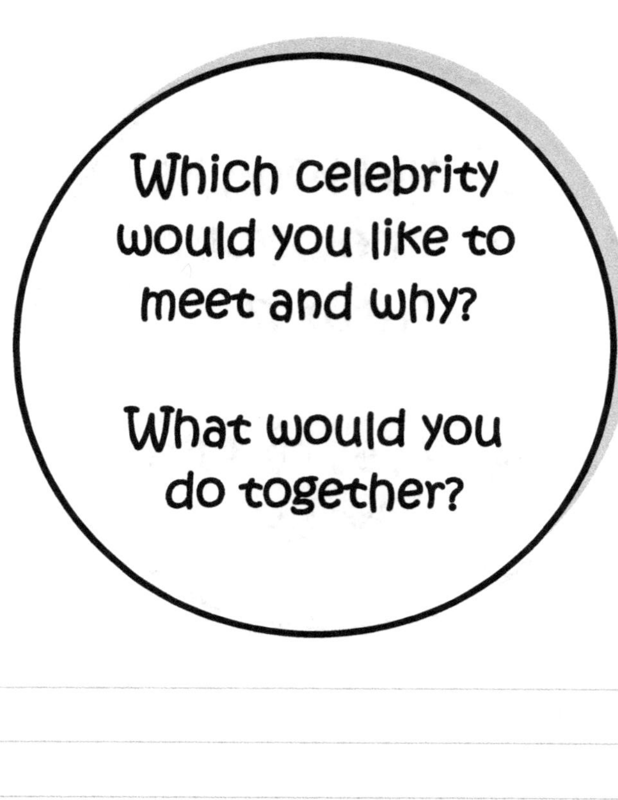Which celebrity
would you like to
meet and why?

What would you
do together?

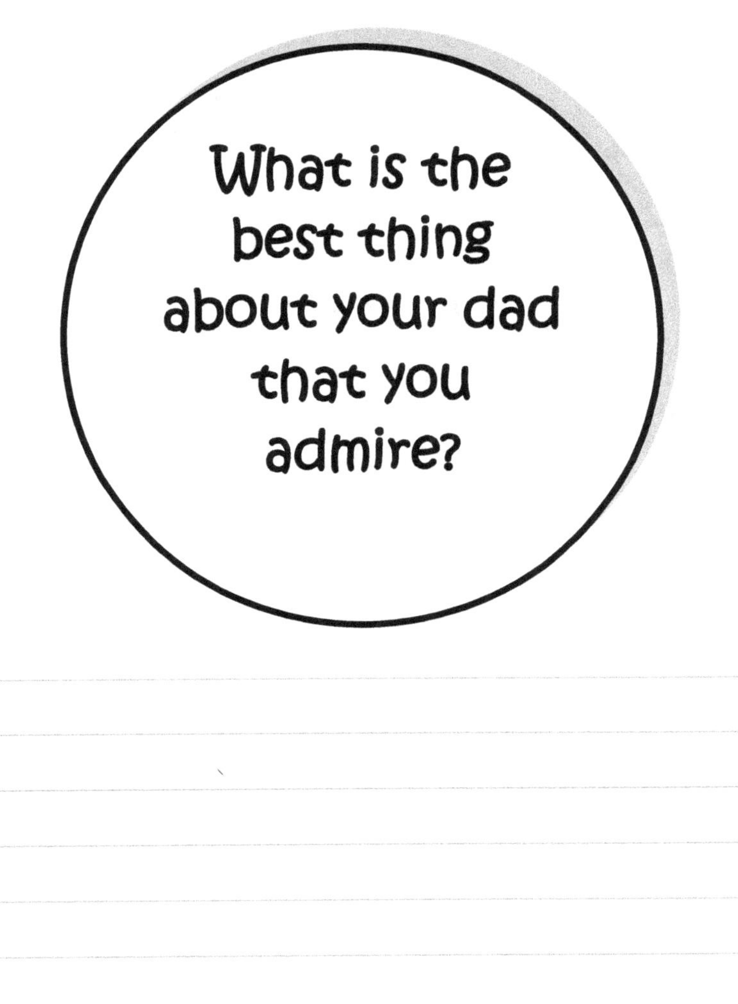
What is the
best thing
about your dad
that you
admire?

What do you
like best to do
with your
mom?

What is the
best thing
that
happened in
your life?

Do you have a
lucky number?
Why do you
think it brings
you luck?

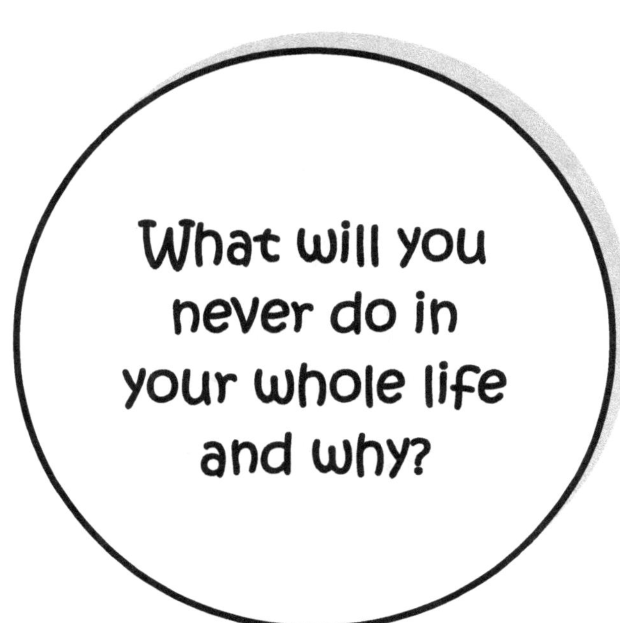

What will you
never do in
your whole life
and why?

What should
they teach in
school or
kindergarten
and they don't?

How would
you
describe
yourself?

Do you believe in
UFOs?
If so, draw on
the next page
what you think it
looks like!

Anything bothering you today?

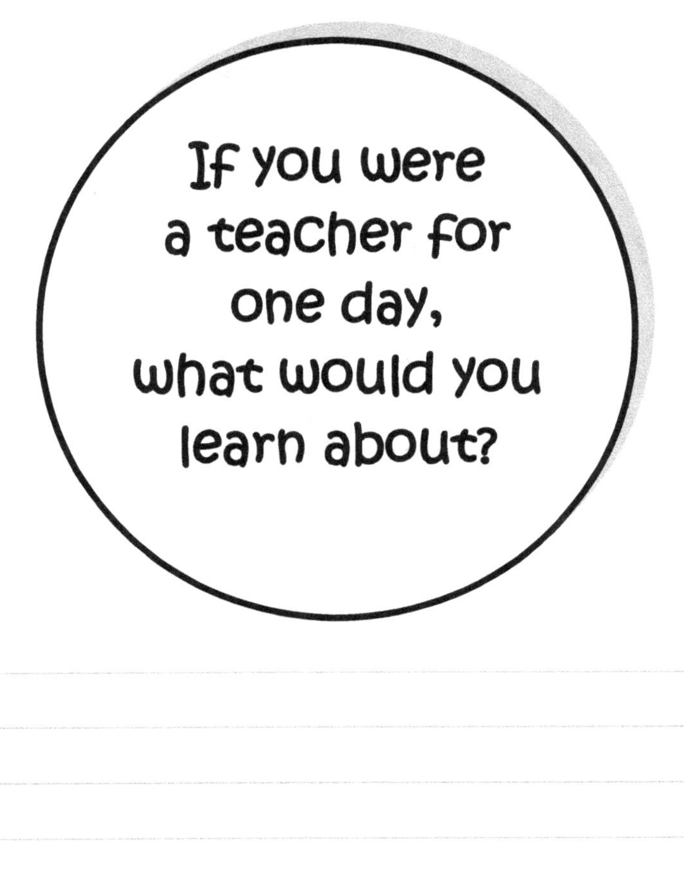

If you were
a teacher for
one day,
what would you
learn about?

Where
would you
like to travel
this year?

Is there
anything
you are
afraid of?

What
is your
favourite
game and
why?

Has anyone
done
something
nice for you
today?

Have you
ever cried
while
watching a
movie?

Have you
helped
someone solve
a problem
today?

Have
you ever done
something
that you are
really proud of?

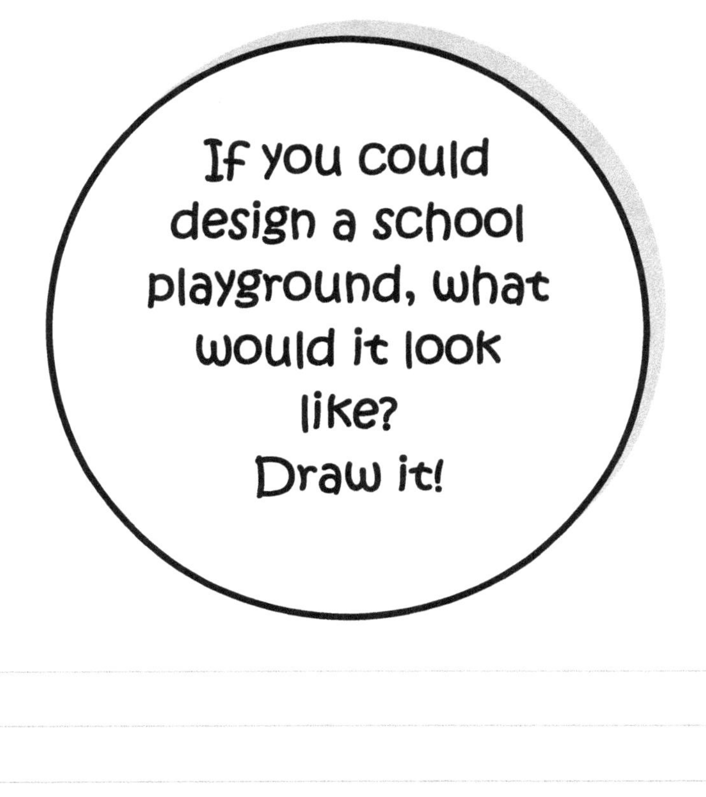

If you could design a school playground, what would it look like?
Draw it!

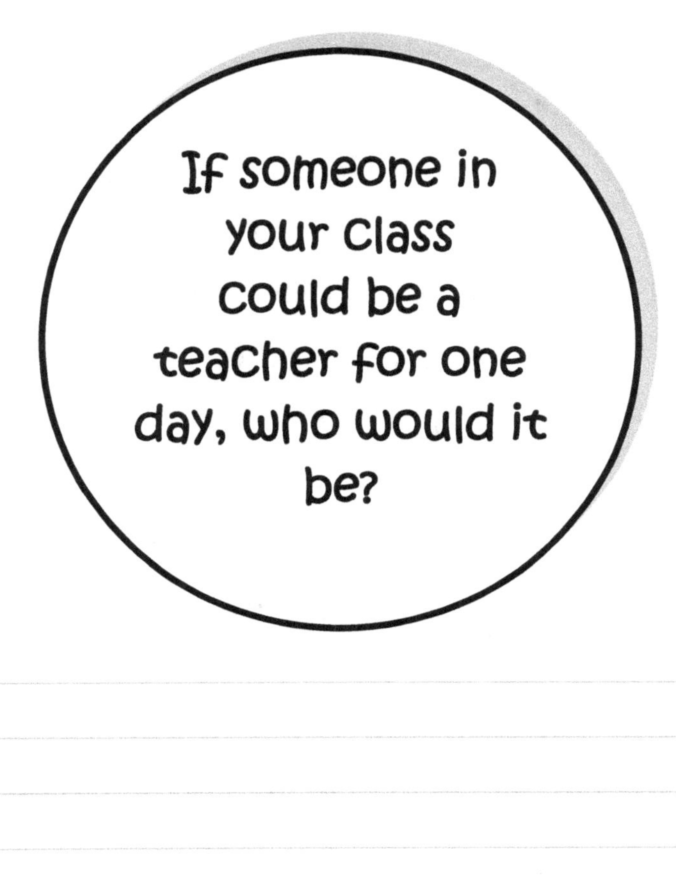

If someone in
your class
could be a
teacher for one
day, who would it
be?

What
would you be
doing outside a
house if you
couldn't get
inside for all day?

If you were
fabulously rich,
what would you
spend your
money on?

If you were a
teacher for one
day, what would
you prefer not to
teach your
children in class?

Did anything
upset you
today?
If yes, what
was it?

If you could use one magic spell in school or kindergarten today, what would you conjure?

If aliens were to take one person from school or kindergarten to another planet, who would it be?

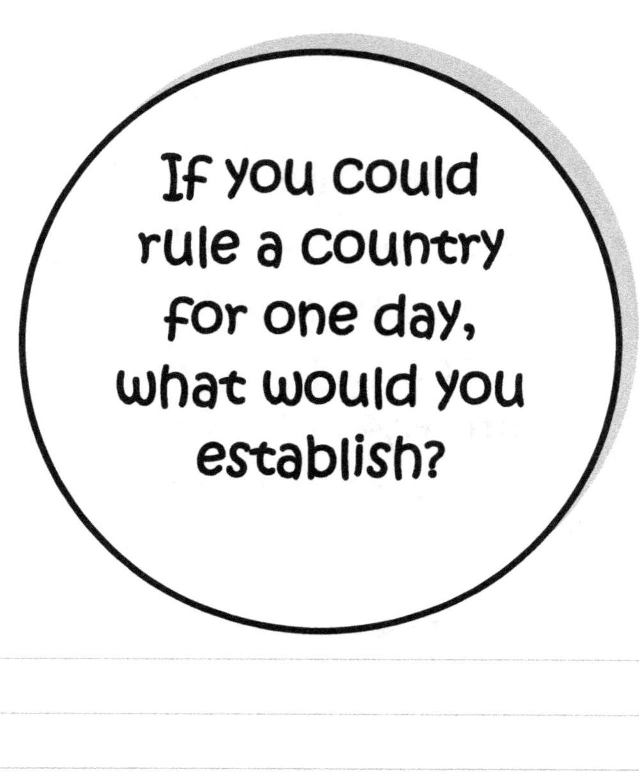

If you could
rule a country
for one day,
what would you
establish?

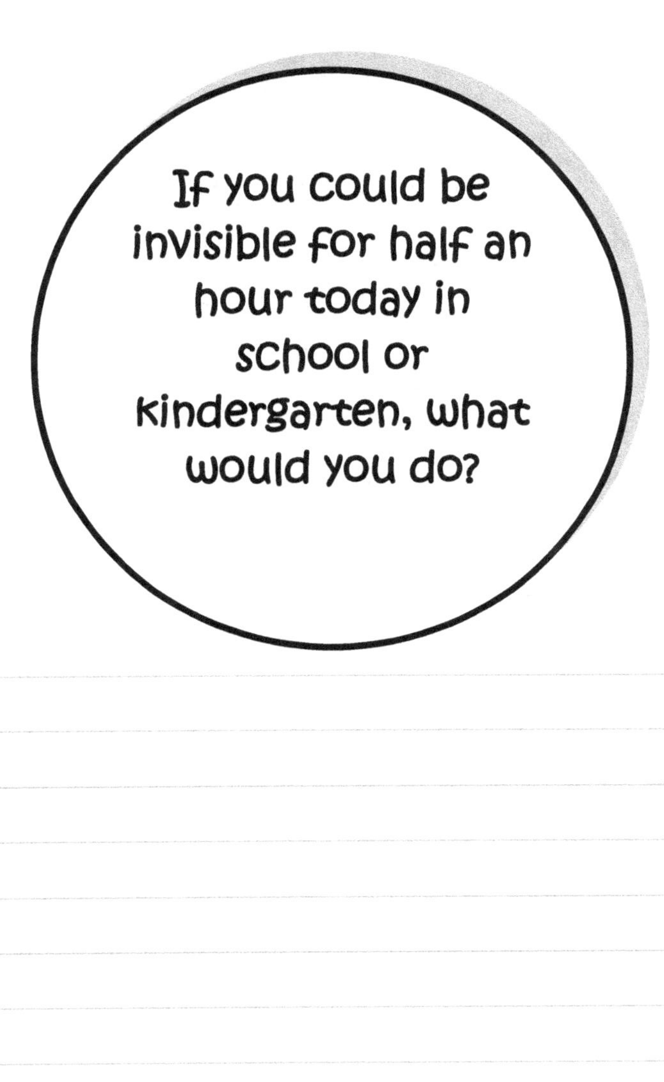

If you could be invisible for half an hour today in school or kindergarten, what would you do?

What would the
walls in school
hallways look like if
you could choose
decorations and
patterns?
Draw them!

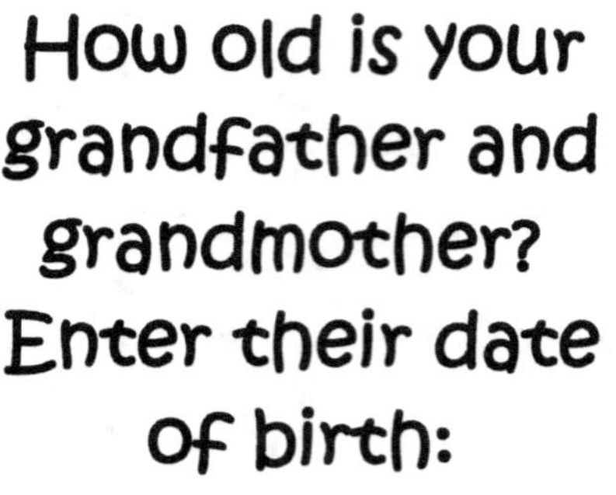

How old is your
grandfather and
grandmother?
Enter their date
of birth:

How many family members do you have?
Count them and write their names:

What would
you name
your dog
or
Cat?

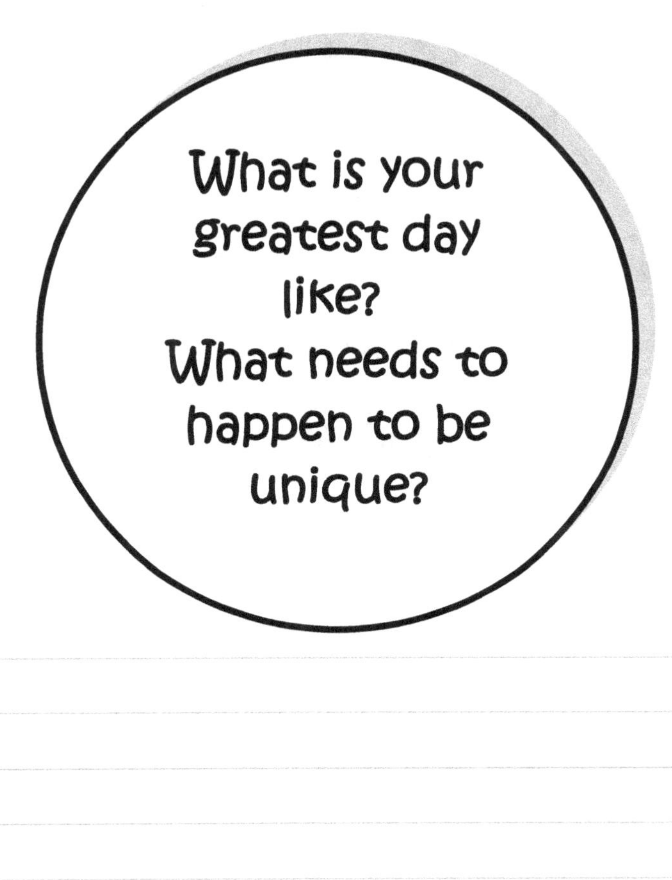
What is your
greatest day
like?
What needs to
happen to be
unique?

Has
something
upset you
today?

What was the
best thing
that
happened to
you today?

What is the biggest
difference between
this school or
kindergarten year
and the previous
one?

What is your
most hated
advertisement?

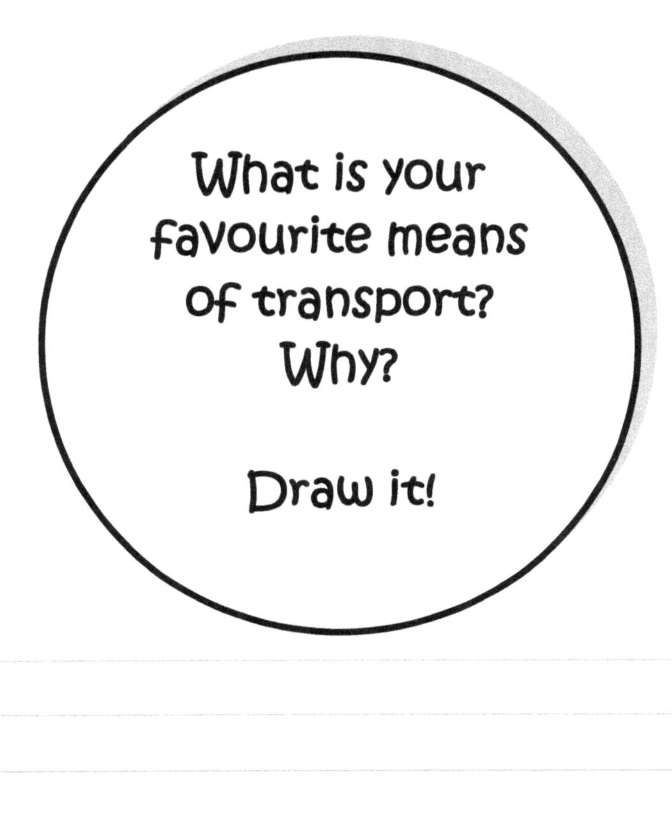

What is your
favourite means
of transport?
Why?

Draw it!

Is there
anything
you regret?

What is your favorite website?

What is
your
favorite
game?

What do you
think is the
worst human
trait?

What kind
of sport
do you like
best?

What thing
would you take
on a camping
trip in the
woods?

What
makes you
happy?

What was your
weirdest
dream
that you
remember?

What is your
favorite
pet?
Draw it!

What is
your ideal
girlfiend or
boyfriend?

What is
your recipe
for a perfect
evening?

What is
your
favorite
fast food?

What is
your
favorite
color? Why?

Who is your favorite teacher? Why?

What is your
favorite
part
of the day?

What is your
favorite
band
or
singer?

What is
your
dream
car?

What is the
best gift
for a teacher
on his
birthday?

Holidays by the
sea or in the
mountains?

Draw your
favourite!

What sounds
make you
happy?
What do you
like to listen to?

What
is your
biggest
dream?

What is
your
favorite
dish?

What is
your favorite
YouTube
channel?
Why do you like
it?

What are the
three biggest
differences
between you and
your best
friend?

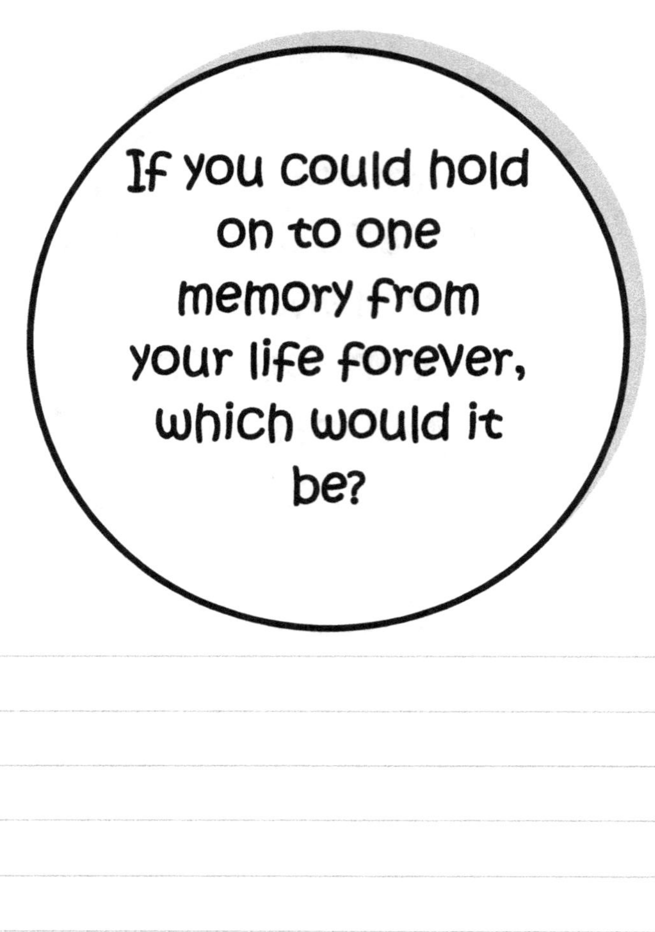
If you could hold
on to one
memory from
your life forever,
which would it
be?

What
animal
is
like you?

What word
did your
teacher use
the most
today?

What
clothes
would you
never wear?

What would you like to get for your birthday? Draw it!

Who do you
want
to
become
in future?

Who is
your
best friend or
colleague?
Why?

Who is your favorite character from books or fairy tales?

Who
of your
friends tells
the funniest
jokes?

When
and where
were you
born?

Which is
your favorite
playground
spot?

Which day
of the week
do you like
best?

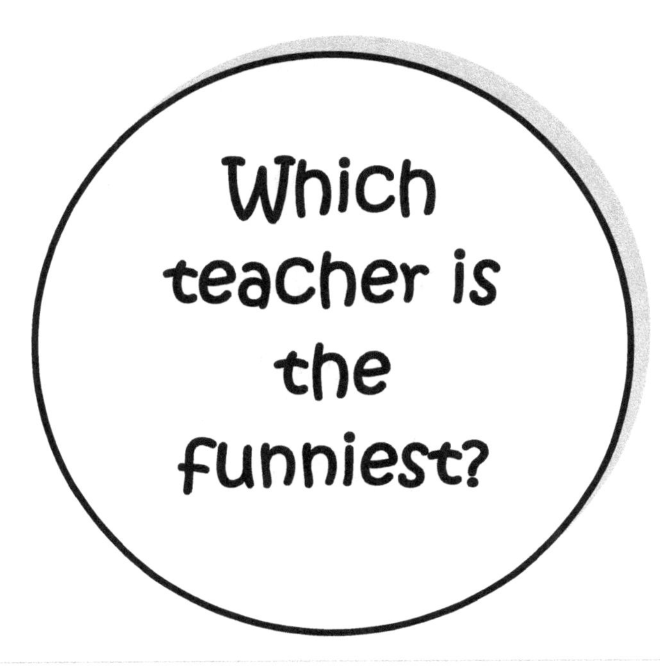

Which
teacher is
the
funniest?

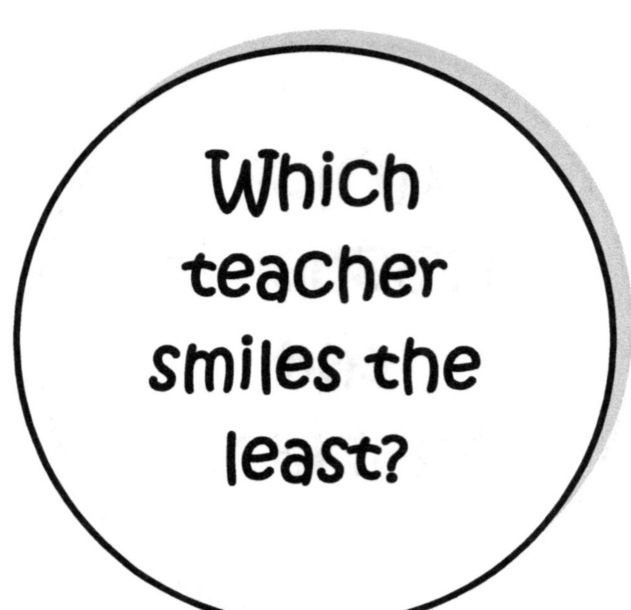Which teacher smiles the least?

Imagine you are going
on vacation to a
deserted island.
Who will you take with
you from school?

Draw a desert Island!

What would
you ask
a goldfish for
if you had
three wishes?

What do you like to do the most while playing in the sandbox?

Did you get
into trouble?
What was the
worst thing you
did?

Have you
ever met
someone
famous?

Did you
hear any
strange
story today?

Did you have a
nickname that
you go by instead
of your real
name? If so, what
was it?

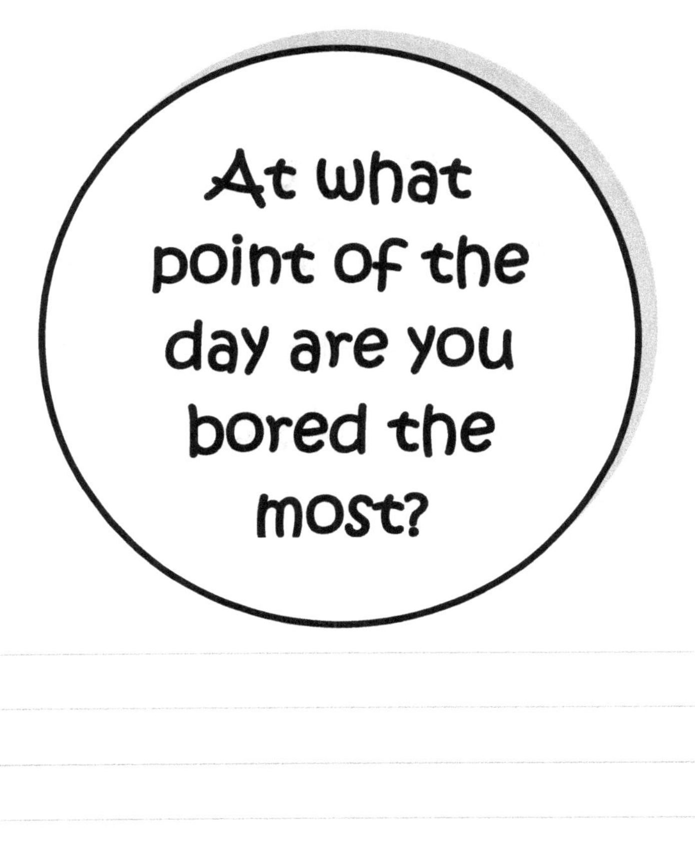
At what
point of the
day are you
bored the
most?

What
smell do you
dislike
the most?

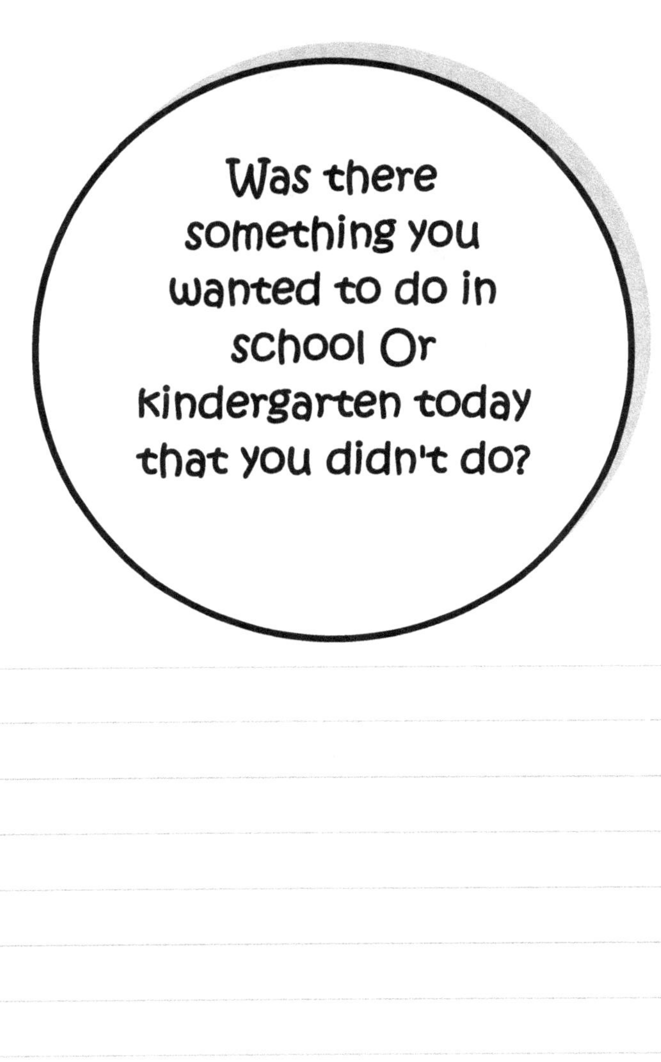

Was there
something you
wanted to do in
school Or
kindergarten today
that you didn't do?

Would you rather have a dog or a cat?

Draw it!

Have you ever
won
anything? What
was it and in
what
competition?

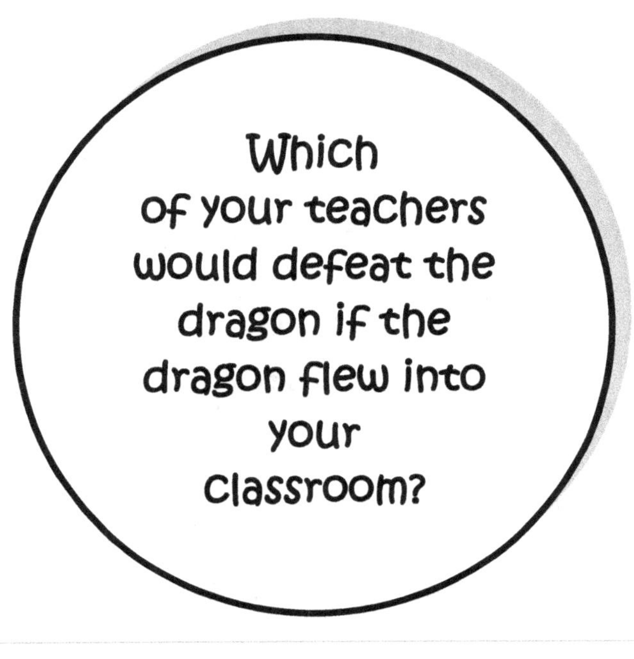

Which
of your teachers
would defeat the
dragon if the
dragon flew into
your
classroom?

Who
did you most
enjoy talking
to today?

If you could
be a girl / boy
for a one day,
what would
you do?

Did you make a
joke or trick on
someone
today?
If so, how?